Abyssinia 1868
Last great expedition of Queen Victoria's Army

Abyssinia 1868
Last great expedition of Queen Victoria's Army

The Letters of

Major Thomas Basil Fanshawe,

33rd (Duke of Wellington's) Regiment

Transcribed by Deirdre Marculescu
Prepared for publication by Derek Alexander

a place of discovery

Valence House Publications

Published in 2017 by Valence House Publications
Valence House, Becontree Avenue
Dagenham, Essex RM8 3HT

www.valencehousecollections.co.uk

ISBN 978-1-911391-04-3

Previous Publications
Sebastopol to Dagenham (978-1-911391-02-9)
A History of Dagenham (978-1-911391-03-6)
The Life of Sir Richard Fanshawe (978-1-911391-00-5)
The Death of the 'Dukes' (978-1-911391-99-9)

Cover Images :
'33rd Regiment at the Magdala Sentry Post'
Regimental Badge
Courtesy of the Duke of Wellington's Regiment Trustees

Thomas Basil Fanshawe (1829 - 1905)

By Mrs Carpenter (1857)

Valence House Museum

These letters were written from Abyssinia by
Thomas Basil Fanshawe
2nd son of the Rev. Thomas Lewis Fanshawe
of Parsloes Dagenham, Essex
He served the whole of his Military Career
in the 33rd Duke of Wellington's Regiment
which included the Crimean War, the
Abyssinian Campaign and Colonial India.
He enlisted as an ensign on the 14th April
1846 and eventually commanded the Regiment
retiring with the honorary rank of
Colonel 2nd March 1878.
Born 3rd Dec 1829 he was married on 8th March
1864 to Emily Catherine, youngest daughter of
Gerard Lipyeatt Gosselin of
Mount Ospringe, Kent
and died 4th May 1905
in Bath where he spent his retirement.

An introduction to 1868 and the letters of Thomas Basil Fanshawe

The conflict between Abyssinia and Britain followed just a decade after the war in Crimean involving most of Europe's great nation states. Forty years of relative peace were shattered by that territorial war, many lives were lost and national finances vastly depleted.

Once peace was regained there was a rapid expansion of trade and industry, propelled by innovative industrial inventions causing most of the continent's major countries to speed towards a more modern age. Ironically, the modern technologies initiated by war spawned a creative fertile seedbed and industry adapted to create fresh new manufactured products that soon became absorbed into everyday use.

Telegraphic cable, so quickly deployed to communicate between London and Crimea, was successfully laid across the Atlantic by the mid 1860's, allowing the readers of national newspapers to expect and rely upon up to date international news.

With a continuous stream of newly patented inventions produced and brought to market, the contemporary population showed little hesitation in accepting and assimilating them into common use. The reaction was little different then from now as eagerly the consumers rushed to buy. Except in those changing times, only few of the population were not obliged to work in factories, or suffer poor living conditions in over-populated growing towns. Yet most were surely exhilarated by the speed of industry's mechanisation.

The wealth of the nation was also changing. New middle classes came to enjoy the convenience and novelty of new forms of transport and housing. No doubt many were aware that the changes they lived through were significant and the most rapid of all previous times.

Reading personal letters and diaries of that time, may help us better appreciate the speed and absorption of these new experiences. Surprisingly, little expression of novelty or amazement is noted and in fact innovative ideas were often treated with a noticeable air of matter of fact.

Appreciating that at this time our own great or great-great-grandparents were young, probably we would be surprised by their level of sophistication. Aware of this when we read the letters from Thomas Basil Fanshawe to his family, he appears very natural and it is easy to empathise with him as he opens a window into Queen Victoria's Army.

Britain was prosperous and enjoying the fruits of an ever expanding Empire but the nation's successful dominance eventually led to the necessity of maintaining a vast peacekeeping standing army across the globe. Successive British governments learnt that careful vigilance was always required to avoid the escalation of local conflicts. This became particularly clear in 1857 when the Mutiny in India almost resulted in total disaster. After centuries, the East India Company was completely disbanded and their old restrictive trading powers swept away.

Radical re-organisation was effected from London and from that time on the British Army maintained a permanent presence in India, re-enforced by newly-formed British Indian Regiments. The two armies ensured effective administration from a strong, direct but benign power.

Recognising that local difficulties needed to be carefully managed, much reliance was placed on subtle diplomacy. It was almost inevitable that eventually a blunder would occur and it came when a relatively minor British Consul in Abyssinia who through a thoughtless act created a crisis. With few political alternatives available to resolve the problem, eventually expeditionary forces were sent to Abyssinia in 1867. The campaign was difficult and arduous for the troops and costly for Britain - perhaps the most expensive of all the Victorian expeditions.

Previously there had been only few minor diplomatic problems between Britain and King Theodore II of Abyssinia and all had been resolved amicably. He ruled his remote kingdom of Coptic Christians peacefully in a realm occupying ancient lands of Ethiopia. Essentially, he was a moderniser trying to bring his newly united kingdom into a strong position within the context of its geographic position on the southern edges of the Red Sea, East Africa.

Mutually good relations relied upon his trust that the British government would aid and re-inforce the protection of Abyssinia if it should be threatened. Surrounded by Muslim neighbours eventually Theodore became uneasy and he wrote confidently to Queen Victoria direct, asking for supplies of weapons and ammunition. He waited for some time without a reply but eventually concluded he was being insulted and ignored.

That was the politically sensitive climate in which Captain Cameron, the local British Consul acted carelessly, bringing about a dramatic situation. Aware that Theodore considered neighbouring Egypt to be an enemy, he insensitively visited Egypt then returned direct to Abyssinia. King Theodore already aggrieved, saw this as a provocative personal affront and retaliated by taking Cameron hostage, together with a number of missionaries and other British nationals.

The Conservative government in London, recognised the hostage-taking as an obvious ploy designed to gain Queen Victoria and Britain's attention and took no action, leaving Cameron and his fellow hostages to their fate.

There was no change in the Government's position for some time but when General Election campaigning got under way the London press whipped up public opinion for the prisoner's plight. As a result, the government pledged to send troops to free the hostages.

By August 1867 a decision was made to send an expeditionary force to Abyssinia under the command of Sir Robert Napier of the Royal Engineer Corps. British regiments currently stationed in India were to be deployed as they were closer logistically to Abyssinia and would be backed up by regiments of the Indian Army.

Sailing from Bombay, the main body of troops left for Abyssinia near to 21st December although Major Thomas 'Basil' Fanshawe and the 33rd Duke of Wellington's Regiment, had already arrived at the destination port of Annesley Bay. Basil's first letter to his mother dated 30th November confirms his arrival on board 'The Indian Chief'. The ship lay in the dock with the regiment on board for several weeks - Basil's letters tells us that Christmas Day was celebrated on the ship. They were waiting the arrival of other regiments and observed vast quantities of logistics and transport livestock, being off loaded onto the dock. All part of a highly organised campaign plan as commissioned by the engineer, Napier.

In Basil's first letter we can sense his anxiety for he suffers from a painful attack of lumbago. The prospect of marching for days and probably months across difficult terrain must have been his concern… As second in command of five companies of the 33rd Regiment he has a staff of 9 officers that he must prepare in anticipation of the arrival of his superior, Colonel Alexander Dunn.

His private thoughts are dominated by Emily (Minnie), his wife. She is alone in India with their two baby sons and needs to organise the family's return to England. His regiment has shipped out quickly and left him no time to take care of the arrangements. How will she pack up their home, sell goods and furniture and organise her

Tewodros II, Emperor of Ethiopia
Giving audience, surrounded by lions
Wikicommons

Sir Robert Napier and Staff
Abyssinian Expedition 1868
The National Archives UK

transport to England? Most married soldiers will probably recognise such situations during their careers.

Basil 'peppers' his letters with enquiries and concerns about the welfare of family members, reminding us that these are intensely personal letters addressed to his mother. He likes to be kept informed and in touch. Through the information he provides unintentionally, he creates a summary of the changes in his family and personal life since returning from Crimea. Clearly, he is no longer a carefree, youthful and optimistic bachelor and there is little doubt that his initial shock on arrival at the front during the Siege of Sebastopol has receded to the edge of his memory. In this second set of his personal letters we find him promoted to Major (18th April 1865), a soberly mature husband and father who is a seasoned officer with nearly twenty years' service and the complications of a young family..

As a veteran of several years 'peacekeeping' in colonial India, he has developed a robust outlook but seemingly remains unjaded by the mundanity and regularity of army routines. The stylish manners that lent him charm in the 'Crimean letters' appear unaffected and fleeting glimpses of his sense of humour still lie between the lines. His relationship with his mother is special and despite his older age and experience he still opens his heart to her. Always waiting to receive her advice he remains unashamed to reveal his sensitivities, hurts and slights.

Basil's natural ability to create vivid images of place and time through his words, cannot alone clarify the many changes that occurred in his family since coming home from Crimea but these additional facts will prepare you for his journey through Abyssinia and his letters:

Basil's father, Reverend Thomas Lewis Fanshawe retired in 1857. The family left their home at Dagenham's old Vicarage in rural

Essex and the Living of Dagenham was sold. The family 'seat,' Parsloes Manor and estate was retained as it had been since 1618. Within a few months of retirement the Rev'd Fanshawe died and Parsloes was inherited by his eldest son, John Gaspard Fanshawe.

Basil's 'dearest mother', Catherine Fanshawe still enjoyed active good health and settled into a London home in Warwick Square. She was close to her daughter Helen and son-in-law Edward Hanson Denison who lived at 33 Warwick Square. Unfortunately in 1864, Edward Denison died and although very comfortable financially, Helen had six children to educate and settle. Basil was close to his sister and maintained a caring interest in her children and was particularly anxious that her sons had successful careers.

Despite or possibly because of his long army career with frequent times apart, Basil shared a lifelong open relationship with his mother. Perhaps blank sheets of writing paper allowed him a way to express his intimate thoughts easier than if they were face to face. His interest and love extended widely across all his family. By making concerted efforts to take a genuine interest in all their activities and well-being he shows not only genuine affection but characteristically a practical approach to maintaining his life away from the detached world of the army. No doubt, from his early youth, when away at Shrewsbury School, he had begun to develop this ability to adapt and compartmentalise his life. That ability must have sustained him during his years of overseas postings.

Almost opposite in character was Dick his younger brother with whom he had attended public school, whilst the older brother John went alone to Eton. Dick chose to drift without a regular career, independently moved in and out of the family's life and often being completely out of touch despite their frequent pleas for news. Remaining unmarried, he later settled in New Zealand.

Through Basil's collected letters from Crimea (published 2016 as 'Sebastopol to Dagenham') we came to know his family and although matured by another ten years, the letters from Abyssinia confirm their personal characters as unchanged.

The letters were intended for his mother and naturally, we only have Basil's view. Unfortunately Catherine Fanshawe had no need to keep her own letters to Basil, but his responses provide many clues to what must have been communicated in the missing half of their correspondence and letters written from India ten years after these from Abyssinia continue to affirm that as the family aged their characters evolved as you would expect.

Individual lives in the family changed but the family estate at Parsloes remained constant. It was rapidly coming to the stage when upkeep overtook available funds. When John Gaspard Fanshawe inherited Parsloes, it was already a problem that needed a resolution and like his father, and later his own son Evelyn, he continually struggled to find a solution. He no longer wished to live at Parsloes and the family preferred to find tenants to cover the expensive upkeep and repairs, whilst they re-located to London.

How to resolve this problem preoccupied the brothers as it had their father before them. Trying to reconcile their present day interests with their heritage, they shared the weight of obligation to their family's past. The new owner, John Gaspard was not so interested in the country pursuits that were the passion of Basil and his father - they delighted in the rural life and sport offered by the Thames marshlands of the Parsloes estate.

John and his wife Bab (Barbara Coventry) chose to live in Halkin Street, Belgravia which suited his career at the Board of Trade in Westminster and they and their young adult children enjoyed vibrant London society life.

The Tudor age had brought the first of their Fanshawe ancestors to Barking and Dagenham having left Fanshawe Gate in Derbyshire. A continuous line of the family lived in Dagenham until Basil's parents left the Vicarage in 1857. Then the residential link of the family ceased although Parsloes Manor was still owned by the family until the early 20th century. After World War I the land was purchased by the London County Council to form part of the Becontree Estate and a beautiful green public space was created on the site of the house, now called Parsloes Park.

When his parents moved from the Vicarage, the loss of easy access to sport on the Dagenham Marshes together with his childhood family home must have saddened Basil but it came in a period when his life became unusually eventful - a posting overseas to India and shortly after his return, his marriage and a new place to call home - 28 Park Street, Bath.

On 8th March 1864 Basil married Emily Catherine Gosselin of Mount Ospringe, Kent. They were well matched and had the advantage of a shared common heritage. Both the Gosselin family and the family of Basil's mother, Le Marchant were ancient Jersey and Guernsey families and the elite of those islands were all closely connected through generations of marriages. Although we do not know how Basil & Emily became acquainted the society life on the Channel Islands was very exclusive and their introduction on the Islands or in London is possible.

Gosselin is not dissimilar to Gostling also a Guernsey name and Basil's Aunt Mary was married to Colonel Charles Gostling, stationed in Malta during the 'Crimean War'. Basil was close to their children, two girl cousins and a brother Fanshawe Gostling - perhaps an opportunity to bring the couple together came from that direction?

Basil was stationed in Dwarka, India in 1859 as well as other postings in the years leading up to his marriage. Opportunities to find and 'court' suitable young women must have been very limited except perhaps at Malta - a very socially active stopping off point for army officers travelling back and forth to the East.

Several of Basil's young fellow officers of the 33rd Regiment missed their social and family life and they 'sold out' after Crimea to return to civilian life. Those, like Basil who remained, soon became steeped in regimental life and became the bulwark of the Army's strength. All regiments relied upon long service officers but army life brought considerable sacrifices and many lost opportunities for a personal and family life.

Exposure to conflict and extreme climates took a toll on their health yet officers needed to maintain considerable strength and fortitude. Exemplary personal discipline was necessary to encourage and motivate men and their own standards of excellence brought to training, order, and routines, came to sustain Queen Victoria's vast army. Only robust healthy soldiers with resistant constitutions survived in harsh conditions and officers tried to boost unity and good morale through comradery and allegiances that reinforced regimental traditions. Yet, long tours of duty abroad served as a reminder of their absence of normal family life.

The officers alleviated this void by creating a comfortable, companionable company 'mess' and in Basil's letters he demonstrated the importance in his life of fraternal mess friendships. Ignoring hardship and distance from relatives, he actively fostered a companionable society in his mess and regularly shared luxuries and food parcels, just as within his own family. His more energetic contributions were produced by his gun, adding fowl and game to the mess 'pot' to make what he normally describes as 'capital or first rate feasts'…

The importance placed on comradery in the regiments was paramount to maintaining a civilized atmosphere. This extract discovered in 'The March to Magdala' by G. A Henty – published in 1868 confirms Basil's reputation as an expert hunter: *'There is no game here, with the exception of hares, which are very plentiful. Major Fanshawe, of the 33d, went out the other afternoon with his gun, and returned in a couple of hours with a bag of nineteen hares, an almost unprecedented amount of sport for two hours' shooting in an unpreserved country.'*

Census records and army lists of the period show how few married men, commissioned or non-commissioned were in the army. Many officers married and established families considerably later than civilian men. They delayed the 'happy state' until they reached a higher rank or even until retirement was in prospect and the sale of a commission would provide a comfortable life with a wife.

Basil still held the rank of captain when he married Emily but we know from his 'Crimea' letters that he always made careful assessments of his opportunities and chances of promotion. Working through possibilities in his practical way, at 34 years of age he presumably considered his prospects remained good. He probably speculated that the regiment would be posted to India for a long period in the next years and as he had served there before, he felt fairly confident that a life in India would be acceptable to a young women - as a place to make a home and have children.

Emily Gosselin was 30 years old when she married and we must assume Basil was either on leave or had a home posting after the marriage, for Helen, their daughter was born at Bath on 12 March 1865. In the following month Basil was promoted 'by purchase' to the rank of Major and within weeks the couple travelled to India with the 33rd Regiment. In April 1866 a son, Gerard was born at Wanauri Line, Poona and after another eighteen months a second son, Herbert at Kurachee.

Those two little boys spoken of in Basil's letters but it is easy to miss that he does not speak of his daughter. Presumably when Basil and Emily left England, little Helen Maude was so young she did not travel with them. Note that 'May' is mentioned in several letters and if read in context, May is actually Helen. The baby girl had an Aunt Helen and a cousin with the same name, so perhaps Basil's daughter was give a fashionable nickname.

Helen Maude remained in Bath with Emily's parents whilst Basil and Emily were in India and they had not seen her for well over two years when Basil asked his mother for information on 'Maude'. Note that Helen had never seen her brothers, *'I hope that you will have a peep at Maude on your way home, I wonder what she will say to her brothers!'*

Basil Fanshawe probably did not have time to dwell upon these affairs as he prepared for the Expedition. As a professional soldier he must have been absorbed in the spectacle of more than 13,000 men gathering in Annesley Bay. As the regiments arrived, along came up to the minute warfare and the specially commissioned logistics for the 400 mile trek high into unchartered mountains. Engineers arrived in the advance party to commence an inland rail track and the roads that were to be constructed ahead of the moving troops. The terrain was known to be difficult and thousands of animals were brought in to transport all the heavy equipment. Arriving on the quayside in January 1868 were horses, elephants, mules and many other beasts of burden, in numbers that exceeding the soldiers three times.

Basil assembled his own baggage as befitted his rank: '*as Field Officer I am taking two portmanteaus, a carpet bag & bedstead (folding canopy), a cane chair & basin (copper). My clothing consists of: flannel shirts, socks, handkerchiefs, uniform of course. Boots rather too heavy I fancy but they were too good to throw away. A suit of thick clothing what we would wear in England... I am only taking two natives as servant & as butler, as they are called, & a groom. I had to find them warm clothing and three months' pay in advance.'*

Towards the middle of January the troops were on the march and as the road ahead was constructed, they followed. The going was slow, hampered every day by long hours waiting for tents to dry and be packed - cutting short the marching, climbing day. Soon orders came down the line and loads were drastically reduced so that by the end of February, Basil was reporting how his comfort was affected:

'Everyone's kit being cut down to 75lbs weight, including everything and the soldiers to 25lb. I have brought nothing on but a carpet bag & my bedding - no bedstead - & a copper basin trimmed with a leather cover which contained the whole of my washing and toilet arrangements. My guns I had to leave behind, one at Senefe & one at Attegerat. I suppose I shall get them again when we go back, if all goes well – my cooking pots go on a pass mule as we are allowed one to every 6 officers – and as our brandy is drunk, I hope to be able to carry my horse gear on one – tables & chairs out of the question. I only regret my guns & powder shot we left behind. The advantages is that not much packing is required of a morning.'

On the rough track there were *'- a long days walk of 15 miles, of course up & down hill & stiff ones'* yet the sights and views were magnificent and they had the time to notice the landscape *'I saw some of the finest trees I have yet seen, a species of Indian fig tree & picked buttercups, wild roses & jessamine'*.

New to European eyes, they encountered exotic birds and animals: *'Great big fellows the latter, as big as donkeys – baboons, in fact. Lots of fine eagles, hawks, green pigeons & small birds, but I could not waste powder or shot nor carry them'*.

Within the first weeks of the march, the 33rd Regiment experienced a tremendous shock when quite unexplained, their commanding officer, Colonel Dunn tragically died. His death left confusion and doubt affecting the morale in all ranks of the regiment as Dunn was a particularly distinguished hero of the Crimean War, awarded the VC, large in stature and in character.

Basil Fanshawe shared a tent with Colonel Dunn and knew him as well as anyone in the 33rd. The nights were cold and sleep was not always easy - there must have been conversations.

Surprisingly Basil has left no information about the event and we can learn little of Basil's emotions about this tragedy from his letters. In the sequence of letters, there would appear to be space for an additional letter, and there can be little doubt Basil requested his mother not to keep that particular letter. It is impossible to imagine that Basil did not tell his mother of the event and what he knew, but we are left with only brief comments spaced through later letters that allow us to assume some of his thoughts. They are only speculation and more details and a summary of the death of Colonel Dunn is included in sequence between Basil's letters.

The progress of the army is never delayed and the 33rd Regiment moved on: *'I hope it may all be over soon as it is not very comfortable work, the country does not improve as we get further into it, though it may. Uphill, downhill varied with grass plains about 2 or three miles long & half as much broad, in the valleys between the hills'.*

The first British troops arrived at the fortress of Magdala on 9th April and found waiting in the surrounding hills, thousands of soldiers of Theodore's army, armed only with spears. Repelling their attack the British inflicted to devastating effect their artillery fire and naval brigade rockets.

Defeated, the Abyssinians quickly retreated into the fortress leaving the British waiting outside. Next day, the British received two released prisoners who carried Theodore's terms but Napier replied by insisting on an unconditional surrender.

King Theodore's response must have surprised Napier (Basil tells us that was his own reaction) when Theodore gradually released all the European hostages without surrendering or making any terms…

Taking the initiative, the British advanced on the fortified city on 13th April and the Royal Engineers made ready to blow up the gates under the cover of massive artillery - unfortunately they forgot to bring their powder kegs!

Luckily, the 33rd Regiment were leading the infantry attack and two resourceful men found an alternative way into the city and were then able to open the gates. They received the Victoria Cross for that heroic act.

Once the infantry flooded in they were able to reach the second gate and inside found the body of Theodore who had chosen suicide over capture. His last act of defiance had been to shoot himself using a pistol received as a gift from Queen Victoria.

It is well recorded that looting occurred at Magdala but from the outset this had been the intention of the British government for they had sent a representative of the British Museum on the expedition. Basil Fanshawe details the looting that was allowed to occur and how Theodore's treasures were distributed: *'Those who got dollars were allowed to keep them but everything else was ordered to be given up. I had a very handsome state dress of Theodore's but was obliged to return it. The sale of things found at Magdala took place here yesterday and the prices fetched were enormous. There was a gold chalice and gold crown which I should have liked to have had but Holmes who is out here for the British Museum got them for it.'* Those objects are today held in the Victoria & Albert Collection, London and Queen Victoria greatly appreciated the work of Holmes who later held important appointments within the royal libraries.

The V & A Collection also holds the beautiful robes and jewelry of Theodore's wife Queen Woyzaro Terunesh. She was being escorted back to her own native land of Semyen in Tigray but died on the journey.

Basil Fanshawe does not make any mention of the King's widow and her son travelling with the army on the return march from Magdala. The fate of seven year old Prince Alamayou was particularly sad, as although he was brought back to England and Queen Victoria ensured his education and care, his only wish was to return to his homeland. He was never allowed to go and at 18 he died in England.

The route back to Annesley Bay would appear to have been less difficult, no doubt without baggage, ammunition spent and the road already formed, the army moved at speed. Basil Fanshawe's last letter in the collection is rushed but written not long after leaving Magdala.

The 33rd Regiment made haste for home – the regiment must have known they were going direct to England as their wives and children had packed up and gone on ahead. The men had been away two years and more – and Basil Fanshawe was certainly delighted to be on his way home and looking forward to spending time with his growing young family - before speculating where his careers would take him next…

Eventually, he returned to India, but not for several years and then without Emily, who from these letters we can assume had not greatly enjoyed her colonial experience.

The Abyssinia Expedition has been well documented and a good account was published as early as 1868 - 'The March to Magdala' a first-hand account by the war correspondent G. A. Henty.

Basil Fanshawe's fluid and well written letters are from a different prospective – that of a senior officer of the 33rd Regiment and until now, read only by his family. His opinions are those of his time and status and allow the possibility of assessing his character whilst appreciating his very personal experience of the 1868 Expedition to Abyssinia.

The original personal letters were generously gifted to the Fanshawe Collection at Valence House Museum Archives & Local Studies Centre by John Gordon. As a great, great nephew of Basil Fanshawe, John truly keeps alive the spirit of his ancestor - offering his own enjoyment of his family and sharing with others their achievements and memories. For his enthusiasm, his friendship and the opportunity of rediscovering so many fascinating 'forgotten' Fanshawes - my gratitude is immeasurable.

Deirdre Marculescu

August 2017

The Letters

The Elephant Train – Abyssinia 1868
Illustrated London News

Transcribers Notes

Capt. Fanshawe's handwriting is relatively easy to read allowing for the semi transparency of the paper. He has written on both sides of each sheet of paper with ink that is not always consistent and he had a need to be economical as postage was prohibitive. As a consequence he made hardly any attempt to punctuate or paragraph his letters to allow more space.

Lack of punctuation creates a problem with the flow of the letters, when read in the original and an early decision was made to insert punctuation in the transcription for ease and enjoyment of the letters.

No other 'improvements' were necessary, as his spelling was almost perfect and he made very few errors that were not self-corrected. As with all good correspondents he wrote with energy and immediacy.

With patience I have transcribed most of his words, but those that elude me are shown by the symbols below.

[ ]	transcribers addition or comment.
[xxx]	indecipherable word or part word - x relating to approximate number of letters.
( )	comments bracketed by TBF in his letters.

Place Names - mostly verified by maps, but within the letters TBF occasionally uses various different spellings for the same place.

Written by Thomas Basil Fanshawe - to his Mother.
Ship – "Indian Chief"[1]
Wednesday November 27th 1867

My dearest Mother

As you can see by the heading of this, that we are off on that wretched expedition. We arrived on board on Thursday last and left Karachee[2] that same evening.

With a heavy heart did I leave Minnie & the chicks. She bore up pretty well considering & I do trust that she will have a good journey home. I do not know when I shall hear from her. I have applied for a passage for them on board one of the troop ships that leaves somewhere about the 6th January. Some leave Bombay in the month of December. I hope she will get a passage as it will I expect the same thing to be £150 if they refuse or have too many applications & then have to return by the P & O Steamer. By the troop ship £50 would cover all expenses, that's for herself & Mrs Dunlop[3] who accompanies her home as servant. I trust she will go well but I shall be very glad to know when she is safely settled down at Park Street[4].

---

[1] Built in 1826 by Gladstone & Co of Liverpool, 416 tons.
[2] Named 'Karachee' by the Dutch in 1742, over time and with British influences, the name evolved to Karachi. Captured by the British East India Company in 1839, Karachi soon became the capital of the new British India province and strategically placed, it grew to be a hub for transportation services with a port and rail links. From Karachi, the first telegraphic message was sent from South Asia to England in 1864.
[3] The wife of Sergeant John Dunlop, 33rd Regiment.
[4] 28 Park Street, Bath - the home of Emily's parents, Mr & Mrs Gerard L Gosselin.

It was a sore trial parting & leaving her alone but it could not be helped and the only consolation was that she had got over her trouble while I was there & was going on well. If we had gone when first ordered, this could have been the case – Baby[1] was doing nicely & very heavy. Gerard[2] was toddling about all day long. He had been very pretty & perfect, so we thought it was teeth & looked one day when his jaw was stretched and found two on their way. It may be a long time before I see any of them again for all anyone knows.

I am writing this to post at ~~Dotwa~~ where we expect to arrive on Saturday morning. This is a fine large ship & I have five companies on board & 9 officers. We are towed by the "Selsette"[3] on board of which Collings[4] who has been given a Brigade & Lacy & H^D Quarters & 3 Cos.

Col. Dunn[5] with two other companies were to leave Karachee on the Saturday after us in the Madras[6]. He & I are going to live together, & no doubt we shall make it out as well as we have done since we have known each other. I have no doubt he will get a Brigade soon which might be a good thing for me should Cooper[7] not come out & what with the turn of luck I am just now having I do not anticipate

---

[1] Herbert Cecil Fanshawe - born 9th November 1867, served in Royal Engineer Militia - died 1952.

[2] Gerard Lewis Fanshawe – born 24 April 1866 in India, enlisted in the Corps of Engineers, promoted to Major 1902 & died of Maltese Fever (aged 38) in 1904, whilst serving in Malta.

[3] An iron screw steamer built on the Clyde by Tod & McGregor of Glasgow and registered in London with P & O Navigation Co. Ltd.

[4] Brevet Lt. Colonel John E Collings 33rd Regiment - born in Guernsey 1831.

[5] Colonel Alexander Dunn – see 'The Missing Letters' pages 25 - 30.

[6] Built in 1864 by W. Simons of Renfrew, Scotland, for the British Steam Navigation regularly sailed between Burma – Madras until 1884.

[7] Lt. Colonel Arthur Sisson Cooper 33rd Regiment - served in the 27th Regiment in NW Frontier during Indian Mutiny.

SS Salsette

Iron Screw Ship – P & O Steam Navigation Company

Caledonian Maritime Research Trust

'New pier at Annesley Bay 1868'
William Simpson (1823-1899) campaign artist for the Illustrated London News.
Anne S.K. Brown Military Collection, Brown University Library

the slightest benefit in any way from the expedition, rather the converse.

Had this order for Collings brigade come sooner, I should have accommodation on board the "Madras" & Dunn in the "Selsette" & Lacy[1] here, but as it only came out just before we started the assignments were made and would not be altered. The accommodation on board here for officers is very indifferent and though the captain is a willing obliging man and the steward willing to do what he can, they have not been in the habit of carrying troops and are out of their groove & the cooking is atrocious – though the actual material as good as one can expect and perhaps a good preparation for what we may expect on landing in Annesley Bay[2]. The soup they give one is floating in grease, ditto tea & coffee & everything swimming in it. You know I am a pretty good sailor & certainly never ill, but it is not tempting grub & I only eat because one is hungry.

We have had most lovely weather since leaving, a nice cool breeze all day & night & the sea like glass the first two days, afterwards a few waves but nothing to signify in a big ship like this of 1788 tons. Yesterday we had to lay to from one o'clock to five in consequence of something going wrong with the 'Selsette' who is towing us – in her engines, we presume, but we have been progressing smoothly since.

---

[1] Captain Richard Lacy (33rd Regiment) – Promoted to the rank of Major, April 1868.

[2] Sometimes called the Gulf of Zula, the bay lies on the Red Sea coast of modern day Eritrea.

So now to my trouble, I have been very uncomfortable with a pain in my back. I suppose a bout of lumbago[1]. I have been obliged to have had it rubbed three times a day by one of the Hospital attendants with a sharp lotion. It has done some good and I am a trifle better today. I have been regularly crippled with it and once sat on a chair or lay bed could not move without pain – a good beginning for a campaign!

I shall leave this open till after we arrive at Aden & send you the latest news of the Force. I suppose we shall be there a couple of days & a couple more will take us on to Annesley Bay where we disembark & perhaps have something more noteworthy to relate.

Minnie of course was in the same house & intends to remain till she's left for England. I hope we shall not lose very much by furniture & traps, but should not be at all astonished if we are disappointed and not get more than a third of what we gave, luck may turn but it has been a long time about it with me I cannot even hold a hand at whist & latterly gave up going to the whist club at Karachee.

I am taking both guns with me and ammunition to match, with a supply flagon of brandy & a case of preserved meats. Dunn, Davidson, Wason[2] & self, do intend to form a little mess of our own. Though the mess arrangements lack room, I am very doubtful about being able to get the whole of them up on the time scales they allow us as field officers. I am taking two portmanteaus, a carpet bag & bedstead (folding canopy), a cane chair & basin (copper). My

---

[1] Pain in the lower part of the back experienced by most people at some point in life, usually caused by physical effort. Lumbago often occurs in younger adults and although the pain can be intensely acute it normally disappears with rest.
[2] Captain Edwin Sandys Wason (1842- 1880).

clothing consists of: flannel shirts, socks, handkerchiefs, uniform of course. Boots rather too heavy I fancy but they were too good to throw away, a suit of thick clothing what we would wear in England.

My horse is coming on with the rest of the Field Officers' horses in another ship, one I believe Col. Dunn's steamer tows, I hope nothing will happen to him, as let alone being very fond of him, I would not know how I should replace him. I am only taking two natives as servant & as butler, as they are called, & a groom. I had to find them warm clothing and three months' pay in advance.

The Belooch Reg't[1] left Karachee two days before us. Belville[2] who commands is not a bad fellow & with whom I had some good shooting last season. Sir R Napier[3] we hear does not leave Bombay till quite the end of December so we shall have a month to look about us.

I received your letter from (Penlee) dated Oct 17 all right, many thanks for it, I suppose Sir Gaspard[4] has decided the question of Blanche's[5] engagement one way or another in her favour I hope, as

---

[1] The Belooch Battalion recruited Balochi, Sindhi and Pathan - the Balooches are an Iranian race with their own language and live in East Baluchistan, now Pakistan and India. In the time of 'British India' these regiments controlled the 'Presidencies' of Madras, Bengal and Bombay.

[2] Major General Henry Belville (1828 – 1897) 27th (1st Belooch Battalion) Bombay Native Infantry.

[3] Field Marshal Robert Cornelius Napier, 1st Baron Napier of Magdala GCB, GCSI, FRS (1810 – 1890).

[4] Lt. General Sir John Gaspard Le Marchant GCMG, KCB (1803-1874) 3rd brother of TBF's mother – British Army Officer & Governor of Newfoundland (1847 -1852).

[5] Blanche Maude Le Marchant daughter of Sir Gaspard Le Marchant, 1st cousin of TBF.

she appears from all accounts attracted to Captain L.[1] I should assume he will be furious at Johnny's[2] debts and behaviour. I do not see how he pretends to avoid losing his commission & then what will he do? Go to the [beggings]?

I am very much afraid this paper is very like the beastly stuff you got hold of for a month or two. I will try to change it at Aden or rather get some more as stationery shops will be scarce in Abyssinia. I am very glad that Mr Hope[3] is doing so much for Parsloes[4] – in the way of keeping in repair and doing so much to it. I shall only be too glad to go down with you & see the place when I return.

I am sorry you have been laid up with one of your bad colds but trust its departure speedily. My indigestion I am glad to say did not bother me long but was most unpleasant while it remained & I hope I will never be troubled with a return of it.

I am very glad Geraldine[5] & baby are doing well. Dick[6] has I hope written to you again & given a good account of how he is prospering. We have very flourishing accounts of Miss May[7], I should like to see her, over two years now since I arrived in India.

---

[1] Captain Charles Henry Laprimaudaye (1839 -1923) – married at St James, Westminster 1868.

[2] St John Thomas Le Marchant – son of Sir Gaspard Le Marchant, 1st cousin of TBF.

[3] Tenant of Parsloes Manor – Colonel William Hope (1834 – 1909) Royal Fusiliers awarded VC for action on 18 June 1855 at Sebastopol, Crimea.

[4] Manor house and estate at Dagenham in Essex, owned by TBF's father, Revd Thomas Lewis Fanshawe, passed down successively since 1619.

[5] Geraldine Gostling - 1st cousin of TBF & daughter of Charles Gostling & Mary Le Marchant married in August 1865 to Richard O'Grady Haly. He retired with rank of Lt. Colonel, Suffolk Regiment (12 Foot) in 1888.

[6] Richard Fanshawe, younger brother of TBF.

[7] TBF's eldest child, Helen Maude Fanshawe born 12 March 1865 at Bath – died June 1950.

This too is the third time of my leaving it & trust it may be the last. I have no wish to see the country or any blessed thing belonging to it again - I suppose I shall get no letters for six months or so, all going to Bombay. I hope you will see May on your road home. I heard from John & Bab[1] by last mail – here comes the call for lunch so goodbye to my writing any more just now –

Nov.28th - I am going to add a bit more today. As we have made such good time the our Captain says we shall probably reach Aden tomorrow evening and as I know you will like to hear I am getting as forward as I can, not knowing how the mails will suit to catch times – please show or tell John and Helen[2] this in case I have not time to write to either or both.

We have been coasting along the south east coast of Arabia all yesterday & today & a (very) hot desolate part it seems – nothing but sand for distances from shore 15 miles about. The ship abounds in cockroaches, having brought a cargo of rice from China and very fine specimens they are, some of them 4 or 5 inches long without the slightest idea of magnifying these dimensions.

Nov. 30th – We arrived here yesterday about 11.30 & there being nothing to tempt me on shore – with my back, which I am glad to say is much better, I remained on board. I do not know when we shall leave. The Report is that the 9th Light Cavalry have lost 100 horses from some unknown disease which baffles all the skill available & have 80 more horses in hospital. Not a charming prospect for a man with only one horse…

---

[1] John Gaspard Fanshawe (1824-1916) & wife Barbara Coventry – elder brother & sister-in-law of TBF.
[2] Helen (Fanshawe) Denison (1826-1917) - TBF's sister, widow of Edward Hanson Denison (1814-1864).

Sunday Dec 1st - Nothing has been seen yet of the Madras so I am afraid I shall not hear how Minnie is getting on. Letters came from Annesley Bay yesterday, but nothing of importance. Water has been found in abundance, which is a good thing. We sail this afternoon so I do not close this. I think it better to write one letter & ask you to let John & Helen see it, instead of writing & repetition to each. I have not been on shore since arriving, nothing to tempt one & my back was very bad, but today I am glad to say, it is very much better.

Bally[1] is here & Collings has made him A.D.C, a good thing for him, Cooper has not turned up. I hope he may not now. The 2nd Queens who are quartered here, have been very civil to us, asked all to dine on arriving & to become honorary members during our stay here, not a very lengthened one, I sincerely trust this will be the last time of seeing this place, this being the 5th time of passing thro' it.

You had better direct to the Abyssinian Field Force – but I cannot know what the arrangements in the Postal department are at present. Some of you shall have a line by any opportunity.

It will take us about a couple of days to reach Annesley Bay. They say the thermometer is down to 40° at night where previously it was up in the hundreds, I presume we are more likely to be frozen than suffer from the heat.

I must wind this up as the Captain is going on shore & will post this. I have nothing more that I can think of worth mentioning & I have written this in so many interruptions that I am afraid that it will be a disjointed epistle but I have tried to give you as much as I was myself aware of.

---

[1] Captain William Bally, 33rd Regiment, Aide de Camp - mentioned in despatches of the Abyssinia Expedition for 'zeal and intelligence'.

I hope that you will have a peep at Maude on your way home, I wonder what she will say to her brothers!

Now goodbye to all of you, ever dearest Mother,

Your most affectionate son
Basil

Written by Thomas Basil Fanshawe - to his Mother.
Ship – "Indian Chief"
Annesley Bay
Xmas Day (18)67

My dearest Mother

Here I am still on board the old ship & when we are likely to land you know as much as I do. I believe the authorities think that the men are better on board ship than on shore, being cooler & we have been waiting for waterproof sheets for the men & breech-loading rifles[1] which I hear are now somewhere on board the ships in harbour – a great lot of [supplies] have come in the last few days, chiefly mules & stores, no more troops have come in. Sir C Stavely[2] was to return last night from Senophee[3] where he had been to see it and I hear Sir R Napier will be here about the 9th having left Bombay on the 20th.

---

[1] Adopted by the British Army in 1866 the .577 Snider–Enfield was a breech-loading rifle. The firearm action, invented by an American, Jacob Snider, was bought into the Snider–Enfield rifle to replace the Pattern 1853 Enfield muzzle-loading rifle.

[2] General Sir Charles W D Stavely GCB, (1817-1896) appointed by Sir Robert Napier to command the first division of the Abyssinia expedition force, organized the base at Annesley Bay, and conducted the fight on the Arogye plain leading to the capture of Magdala.

[3] Senefe, Abyssinia (Eritrea) - Clement Markham carried out reconnaissance before the British expedition, reporting it was situated "at the foot of the grand mass of sandstone rock about half a mile north-west of the camp, called Amba-Adana." The town itself consisted "of about a dozen houses built of rough stones and mud, with flat roofs, branches being placed in rows across the beams and covered with mud. Broken jars plastered into the roof, serve as chimneys." He gave the population as 240 people. *Journal of the Royal Geographical Society (1868).*

Robert Cornelius Napier, 1st Baron Napier of Magdala

John Watkins - albumen carte-de-visite 1860's

Supply Depot Zula (left)
Duke of Wellington's Regiment Trustees

There are no end of shaves current about the Prisoners[1] being given up but I do not vouch for the truth having come so far. I should like to see what the country is like in the interior. Some of them in Senopfee say it is quite cool, too cold at night & our two companies at Kumaillie[2] or some such district say it is not very hot, they (2 Cos) are about 8 miles inland.

Three companies are on board & employed in the noble occupation of watering the mules, all 3 Cos. just from here, so I have plenty of work for the men left. The "Madras" sent her two companies on board the "Selsette" where Col. Dunn & HO Quarters now reside. I shall not be sorry to get on shore.

I am very sorry to tell you that we have lost an officer, Capt. Smythe[3] poor fellow, we buried him yesterday morning on shore. I am afraid his attachment to the bottle was the significant cause. Yesterday I was busy all day, taking an inventory of his kit, of course you must not say what he died of! Jervis[4] gets his company on tenant purchase for which he offered Smythe £800 over regulation, not 3 months back but the registration fell thro! The Horse Guards sent an official to say that Cooper had got further leave till January 29th from Medical Board when if he was not well enough to come out & join, steps would be taken to replace him by an efficient officer. Anyhow, if he does not come out I must benefit by the exchange that will probably take place. I think it about time I

---

[1] Emperor Theodore of Abyssinia imprisoned missionaries and representatives of the British government in an attempt to gain the attention of the government in London, when it became apparent that military assistance would not be offered to his country.
[2] Kumayli – approximately 15 miles from Annesley Bay.
[3] Captain J C Smythe, Quartermaster (Abyssinia Regimental War – York Minister).
[4] Captain Edwin Jervis, later of the 8th Foot Regiment.

should have a turn, I fancy Dunn will go as soon as this affair is over, so it would be a good thing if Cooper could not return to us.

Now let me thank you for your letter of Dec 2nd which reached me on 19th , I only received before that on arrival, one, so I wondered as you say you have written three, then the second has been missed. I have since received one you enclosed to Minnie and two others, one from John & the other from Aunt Caroline[1] to Minnie which ought to have gone to Kurrachee but got no further than Bombay because my name was on them. I was very much disgusted and annoyed the other day to find a letter I had written to Minnie being put into my hands for troops directed to 33rd Depot, Kurrachee …….it only got as far as Bombay & come back – a great nuisance & now I cannot know if she will think of asking at the Post Office at Suez or Aden[2], besides she will think all sorts of things. I heard from her dated on the 9th, she was going on all right, but found it very dull.

I almost hope they will refuse her a passage home in the transport of 6th January, as Sinclair[3] heard from his wife, and she says they are most uncomfortable, that children have nothing given them in the way of food from 5 o'clock at night till eight next morning, to add very crowded. Ladies only allowed beer at lunch or dinner, not both, a little claret and a glass of sherry afterwards, certainly not liberal & children not allowed to sleep in the cabins with the

---

[1] Caroline Le Marchant Somerville (born 1802), sister of TBF's mother and widow of Captain John Somerville (1796 – 1852) Royal Artillery - lived at Heavitree, near Exeter, Devonshire.

[2] To avoid the long sea voyage around the Cape of Good Hope before the opening of the Suez Canal in 1869, the journey back to England involved travel by sea from India to Aden, then a journey north by land to Suez on the Mediterranean coast and from there another ship to England.

[3] Surgeon Major James Sinclair MD – 33rd Regiment (1832-1910) - later Principal Medical Officer in Malta and promoted to Surgeon General – Principal Medical Officer for Ireland - retired 1892.

mothers, only in the nurseries. The arrangements seem to be on the principle of how to make every one as uncomfortable as possible. I hope she will have heard in time, so as to get off by the P & O boat on the day after tomorrow from Bombay (27th) but I doubt it. I hope if she goes by transport that it may be a more comfortable ship & a more civil Captain & have no trouble with the children.

I trust you found Maude blooming and not forgotten you, what will she say to her brothers? I have no doubt there will be great rejoicing when they arrive safe in Park Street.

The heat is very great again yesterday & today – till the breeze spring up!

Did Aunt Caroline write to me, do you know for I have received no letter, though I got a letter intended for Minnie from Aunt C.? I am glad she likes the shawl and cushions, did you see them and what did you think of them?

So Sir Gaspard has consented to Blanche's engagement, what has he done about Johnny's affairs? I am much obliged for Sir G. writing to Sir R Napier but fancy I shall not expect much benefit from it, pray thank Sir G. for his kindness.

I am glad that a start of sort has been made at the Docks[1] and hope it may prove the beginning of a prosperous concern. I hope that you

---

[1] *'An abortive scheme for a dock at Dagenham, linked by railway to the existing line at Chadwell Heath, had been proposed in 1846. The idea was taken up again in 1854 by Sir John Rennie (1794–1874), and others. Two Acts, of 1855 and 1862, gave powers to connect Dagenham Breach to the Thames by means of a lock, with a railway to the newly-built London and Tilbury line. In 1865, after several unsuccessful attempts, a company was formed for the purpose, work started under Rennie's direction, and a pier was built, but in the following year the contractors got into difficulties and could not continue. In 1866*

have heard from Dick that he received the money and done well with it, he seems a long time in saying anything about himself. Helen has got rid of her cold by this and having a merry Xmas with all her boys with her – this does not seem much like Xmas weather - with us – what the heat must be in the hot weather, I cannot imagine and should not care to be here.

John & Bab I conclude are in town and have all their ~~houses~~ belongings with them. The two houses, if they dine together will make a large party and no doubt you will be of the number. I am going to ask John to do for me a little coming home order for the Field Newspaper[1] to come out regularly £1-6s for a year, I think. If John will pay for it, I will ask Lizzie[2] or Minnie to repay John at once. I ought to receive it every week as Bengal & Bombay mails bring our letters & it is about the only paper that I care about seeing that I do not see, the mess not taking it in.

What a mistake Johnny Thomas[3] seems to have made with his wife, in fact neither appear to have done well.

---

another Act was obtained, with wider powers, but no further action was taken, and in 1870 the company was liquidated' (Victoria County History – Essex). Sir John Rennie was known to TBF's father and the family's money had been invested in purchasing additional land in this area in anticipation of the venture.

[1] 'The Field' is the oldest country newspaper in the world and has been published continuously since 1853. It was created by Robert Smith Surtees as a paper for sportsmen, landowners and farmers as well as for high society. It has supplied a view of all important in the sporting world, especially the unusual and eccentric whilst at the same time, it has been at the forefront of a great many causes that improved or regulated country life.

[2] Elizabeth C Gosselin (1830–1905) unmarried elder sister of TBF's wife Emily, living at the family home in Bath.

[3] St John Thomas Le Marchant, later Colonel, Royal Horse Artillery, son of Thomas Le Marchant (youngest brother of TBF's mother) - married Agnes Maria Purcell on 20th November 1866. Daughter of Sir J H Lethbridge, and widow of Peter Valentine Purcell, Captain 13th Light Dragoons (married 1855 - died 1864).

I have no news to give you except water continues hence and not preserved from the ships condensing, the railway[1] is making a little progress & is very promising. Did you see those sketches of the papers in the Illustrated London News[2]? Pleasant looking spots to pass through with an enemy in possession, all they have to do is cast down stones from the top.

I have to write to Bath & Minnie – so with much love to you & wishing I was with you instead of sweltering out here. My horse is not looking half as well as he did – I hope he won't get sick & drop off, a vicious disease is prevalent here which no one seems to have any knowledge of - among the mules & horses. They fall sick, drop down & die with a mass of froth issued from mouths & nostrils and when opened, the whole of the interior a honey combe from some small creature which is supposed to have been swallowed in the waters.

Once more, Goodbye, ever dearest Mother

Your affectionate son
Basil

How is Mrs Russell[3] getting on? I suppose a boy would have been a more pleasing arrival[4].
Tell Margaret I asked after her.

---

[1] The railway being constructed by the Corps of Royal Engineers ahead of the troops to transport the equipment and supplies from the port across the plain.

[2] Published from 1842, The Illustrated London News was the world's first illustrated newspaper.

[3] Mrs Emily Russell, wife of Champion Russell – living at Stubbers, North Ockendon, Essex a distance of no more than 5 miles from Parsloes, the Fanshawe family home at Dagenham. Mrs Fanshawe frequently visited this family, and in 1871 she was registered as a 'visitor' in the census return for the property.

[4] The birth of Lilian Russell born during the last quarter of 1867.

Written by Thomas Basil Fanshawe - to his Mother.
Camp Youlla
Thursday January 2nd (18)68

My dearest Mother,

The Mail leaves tomorrow and I leave tonight with three companies for the first camp in route to Senefe. I suppose will be 5 days doing it. We landed from the "Indian Chief" on Saturday morning & the H^D Quarters at the same time and I have been full of work ever since. It is cooler on shore than on board ship and I am infinitely better for the change. This morning we had rain for an hour but the sun has come out again & it is hotter than usual. I very much doubt getting all my troops up with ease but must trust to luck. I have very little news since I wrote last, the mail from England came in two days back but brought no letters for any one – I have not heard from Minnie again so you know as much about her plans as I do. I heard last night that the troop ship Jumna has been delayed & instead of leaving Bombay on the 6th of January, she won't be away before the 21st. I hope Minnie will not wait but go home in a P & O boat. She will be so much more comfortable than on board a transport for the arrangements are anything but pleasant, as I think I told you.

Sir R Napier is expected here either today or tomorrow and then we shall see what is to be done. Some say that he won't come from Senefe till he has got 6 months' supply of stores there, others think he will push on with flying columns[1] as fast as he can. The prisoners are still at Magdala & everyone seems to think that either they will

---

[1] Military term for a small, independent land unit, usually less than the strength of a brigade which is capable of rapid mobility and deploys minimum equipment and is often formed in the course of an operation.

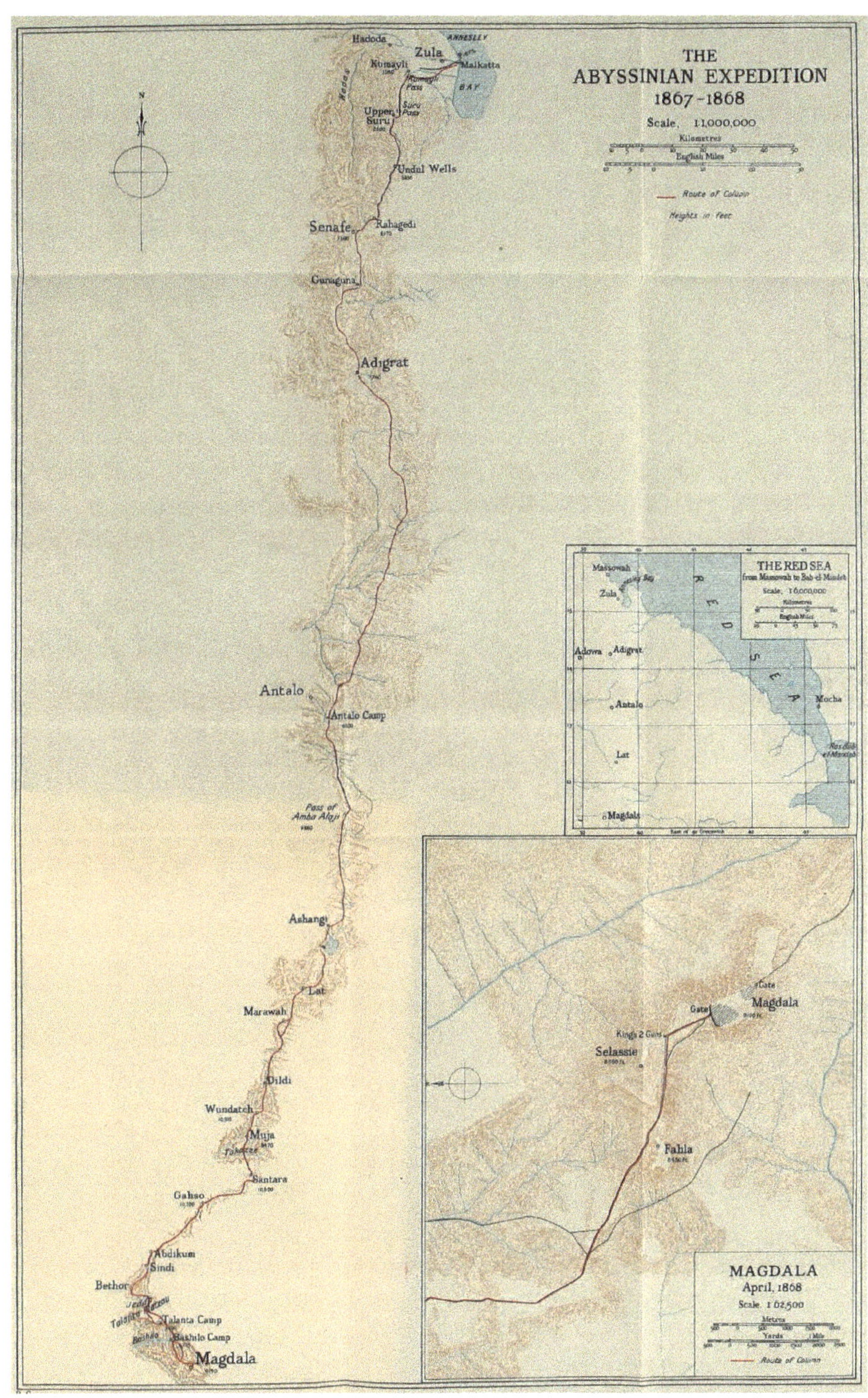

Abyssinian Expedition 1867 – 1868

Campaign Map

Maps & Plans – Fortescue's History of the British Army (Volume XIII)

Senafe Encampment

Duke of Wellington's Regiment Trustees

be given up by the Prince of Tyre - or Theodore[1] will if he gets them again, give them up. I expect we shall have a lot of hard work marching with very little luggage. Some say that the expedition will last two years, others that it will be over by May next. I devoutly hope the last may be true. Three companies have gone on from us, including two landed first. I go tonight with Irvine[2] & Dunn with H^D Quarters will follow in a couple of days next. I shall not be sorry when we arrive at Senefe. The road[3] I believe is pretty good now and in another 10 days will be fit for wheeled carriage & artillery. The 4th Regt[4] arrived some three of four days back & are still on board ship & land when we depart. We have got our new blankets & breech loading rifles and so are ready now.

Last night we had quite a large party to dine at our little mess which is comprised of Sinclair, Wason, Dunn & self. We had Doctor Currie[5]

---

[1] Téwodros II (translated to Theodore) - born c1818 - Emperor of Ethiopia from 1855 until his death in 1868.

[2] Possibly Major Irvine of the Royal Artillery.

[3] The advance party of The Corps of Engineers constructed a road that would climb to <u>Senafe</u> – a route of more than 60 miles – this would accommodate not only the troops but also the carts and carriages transporting their equipment. It was also necessary to provide safe footage for the elephants carrying the rockets.

[4] 4th (King's Own) Regiment of Foot.

[5] Surgeon General Samuel Currie, C.B., M.D., Q.H.P. (*extract: British Medical Journal 1898*) 'The death of this officer at the age of 82 removes the oldest officer (except one) of the Army Medical Department. He studied at Edinburgh University, where he graduated M.D. in 1835. He entered the army October, 1836, retiring in 1876 after forty years' service. He served with the 16th Lancers at the battle of Maharajpore in 1843, and afterwards in the Sutlej campaign of 1846, including Aliwal and Sobraon and other actions (bronze star, medal, and clasp). He was Field Inspector in the China campaign of 1860, for which he was made C.B. (medal with clasps). He was Principal Medical Officer of the Abyssinian Expedition of 1868, for which he was promoted to the rank of Inspector-General of Hospitals, mentioned in dispatches, etc. (medal and clasps). His final rewards were the title of Queen's Honorary Physician, a good service pension, and lately the Jubilee Medal'.

the head surgeon of the doctors, a Dr Martin[1], Col. Wood Asst. Adjutant General & another two. I got away early, in bed by 9 o'clock, early hours being the order of the day and was on parade at 6 this morning and marched the regiment out for a walk & came across 4 bustards[2]. Of course, I had no gun & they were a long way off.

We hear that the 2nd Division in which the 26th & 45th are, have been counter commanded for the present. Things are not very easy here as I told you before, our little mess had the precaution to bring three boxes of preserved meats[3] & very useful they have proved, for we get nothing but our rations of 1lb of bread and & 2 drams of spirit – not being a beer drinker I don't miss it for it cannot be got. I do not miss it as much as others. For the first time three days we got porter[4] but that soon ran out.

My horse is all right and I hope will remain so, one good thing, last night in orders, it appears that officers losing their horses are to have them replaced from the Land Transport Corps[5], so we shall not be

---

[1] Assistant Surgeon Martin.

[2] Bustard – from approximately 1830 this bird had been extinct in UK but in recent times, within the last 20 years a similar species from Russia has been successfully re-introduced.

[3] Expanding beef production in the US, Argentina, Australia and New Zealand led to a race to invent the most hygienic, tasteful and efficient methods of curing and preserving meat. In Argentina a prize of $8000 was offered as part of a worldwide search for the best system that could be brought into mass production.

[4] A dark beer specific to London, made from brown malt, reputedly named Porter after the street & river porters with whom it was popular, it originates from the 18th century and remained popular until the late Victorian period.

[5] The Land Transport Corps formed in 1855, became the Military Train in 1856 then soon after the Army Service Corps. The Corps was responsible for land, coastal and lake transport, barracks administration, the Army Fire Service, staffing headquarters' units, supply of food, water, fuel and domestic materials such as clothing, furniture and stationery and also the supply of technical and military

moved to walking in the event of our losing our animals from sickness or any other cause. Several have already died, though none of ours.

I am very anxious to get another letter from Minnie, to hear how she and chicks are getting on & when they leave for England. I drank theirs & all your healths last night and hoped that next New Year's Day we might be all together for I do not fancy, if this expedition is over as early as May – they will send us back to India.

I hope you heard from Dick & that he gives a good account of himself. How did you find Miss May on your way home through Bath?

I have all my things to pack for the march, & no time – so wish best love to all!

Believe me ever dearest Mother, your most affectionate son

Basil

---

equipment. By 1880 the name had evolved into the Commissariat and Transport Corps and today, it is the Royal Logistic Corps that maintains these responsibilities in the British Army.

Written by Thomas Basil Fanshawe - to his Mother.
Camp Senafee
Tuesday January 13th (18)68

My dearest Mother,

I will begin my letter to you today as I believe the last safe date to send after from here, to catch the mail leaving Annesley Bay on the 20th, is the 17th. You will see from the heading that I have arrived so far up the country. I left Zoulla on the 3rd got to Kumaglia, a march of about 19 miles, the same morning & halted there with 3 companies till the morning of the 5th. We had heavy rain that night so had to wait till the tents were dry which was not till near two o'clock midday. We got to Upper Seroo about 6.30 & from Upper Seroo to this place is nothing but a pass through magnificent scenery of grand mountains but it feels very monotonous after the first day's march.

From Upper Seroo we marched the next day to a place called Undel Wells & the next to a place called Rauefuddy[1] – a long march of 18 miles good – the march from that place in Senefe is the prettiest of the whole. The road all along is very stony – but what it must have been before the road was made? Must have been a caution – even now it is little more than the bed of a torrent with the big stones taken away. About 3½ miles from Senefe is the worst piece of road, a regular hill side but they are making a zigzag road as far as practicable.

---

[1] Rahagedi (*Abyssinian Campaign Map 1867-1868*).

Sir R Napier arrived the day I left and I believe is coming up here shortly, General Malcolm[1] who commanded our Division, we believe arrived yesterday in camp. We are encamped on a plain with hills all around us & beastly cold it is at night, the thermometer going down to 36° & 38°, & 90° in the sun in the day – rather a joke is it not with a cold wind blowing. Every person's hands & faces are chapped & blistered from the continued effects of wind & sun.

We know nothing of when we shall move on, though there is a report that the 10th & 25th N.I. Rgts[2] are to move on to make roads – in advance in the course of a day or two. We hear that King Theodore is trying to reach Magdala & get the prisoners into his power but he does not make much progress – a mile a day, being harassed by what he calls the rebels. Reports say Sir R Napier won't move till he has six months supplies here which will take a long time to accumulate owing to the Land Transport arrangements which are lamentably bad. The mules or camels are sent down without any responsible person in charge and the mule drivers are the scum of the earth - Arabs, Turks, Maltese, Egyptians and not a word of their language can you understood nor make then understand you – besides the animals are often as not without ropes or straps to the stools on which or rather to which to pack the tents & men's tents over & it is a severe trial of patience getting the baggage started on the march. They say, when we leave this, we will only be allowed one mule per officer.

---

[1] General Sir George Malcolm KCB (1818–1897), commanded the second division, which guarded the line of communications.
[2] North India Regiments.

I must try & buy myself a tattoo[1] somewhere.

My horse so far is all right and I believe after being here 10 days they are considered safe. We came in on the 9th last Thursday – Lacy lost his charger at Undel Wells and walked the rest of the way. I have been out shooting twice for an hour or so – the first time I did not actually see a thing to fire at. On Saturday last, I went out with two others, we got three or four brace of partridges & a guinea fowl. We shoot not entirely for the pot as with our large numbers, nearly 31 in mess, the consumption is great. The shooting is uncommonly hard work – up the side of hills like the side of a house on loose slippery stones with a patch of jungle here & there. The birds always seem to choose the moment to rise when you are in a nastier place than usual, I had six shots at partridge & killed five but only bagged two, very bad luck. I had a long shot at a deer which missed, I fancy – at any rate did not get him. This place is about shot out and I do not care how soon we move on to where game is more abundant.

I got all my ammunition & guns up all right and only hope I may be able to take them on all right. The Col. (Dunn) & I are living together in the same tent, at night we have enough to do to keep ourselves warm.

____

[1] During the 19th century, the British Army approved and encouraged tattooing. The Prince of Wales (Edward VII) had several tattoos and made it a fashion among the gentlemen of London Society. Field Marshall Earl Roberts who was himself tattooed - stated that "every officer in the British Army should be tattooed with his regimental crest. Not only does this encourage esprit de corps but also assists in the identification of casualties".

I cannot say much for the beauty of the natures of either sex that I have come across. I do not know if they will improve as we get further into the country.

The Postal services[1] seem to be on the happy go lucky principle. I got two letters from Min – one dated 13th and one dated 24th December two days running, and the last came first. She did not know if her passage had been granted in the Transport that was to sail next from Bombay. I hope she & the chicks are well on the way home & they will have a good passage.

People at Karachee do not seem much disposed to be civil to Min. The Styles being the only ones that called & done what they could. Though several promised promises, easily made & soon forgotten.

Our depot is to go home from Karachee as soon as arrangement can be made for their departure, lucky people!

Some people say we shall be here two years, I sincerely trust not but I cannot see much chance of it being over before May as some people anticipate.

There are some very lovely birds, like humming birds, on the way up, but rather bigger – that flash in the sun[2], all with colours & no end of baboons, some of them great big hairy beasts[3], & hideous as

---

[1] Prior to this conflict there had not been an official postal service. Sir Robert Napier initiated the service using overprinted Indian stamps.

[2] Some of the 23 species of brightly coloured Sunbirds found in Abyssinia.

[3] The Gelada (*Theropithecus gelada*), sometimes called the bleeding-heart monkey or the gelada baboon, are found only in the high grassland of the deep gorges of the central Ethiopian plateau. Being large and robust they are covered with buff to dark brown, coarse hair and have a dark face with pale eyelids. They live in elevations 1,800–4,400m above sea level, using the cliffs for sleeping and grasslands for

possible. I suppose we shall see more strange animals as we advance, & hope some may prove useful for the table – our rations are only 1lb of meat & 1lb of bread, with a certain amount of vegetables (preserved), tea, pepper etc.

I must stop for the day & finish another time as I am called off.

Wednesday 15th – I am told that today is the last day for posting, as it sometimes takes 4 days to reach Zoulla. I think I answered your last in mine of January 2nd. The Col. has had a touch of fever yesterday & I have been touched up a little with diarrhoea but I am much better today – the effect of change of climate & every one suffers more or less. I have no news & lots to do as Commanding Officer pro tem.

Love to all, I shall begin & number my letters home, so keep the envelopes or note the numbers to see if you get them right. I never got your second letter that you said you wrote, but I am not surprised at it. Hope you have had a letter from Dick & he is going on all right.

Goodbye, Dearest Mother, with best love to all,

Ever your most affectionate son
Basil

Tell John I will look out for feathers for him here!

---

foraging. Geladas are the only primates that are primarily graminivores and grazers with grass blades making up to 90% of their diet.

'The Missing Letters'
(note from the Transcriber)

The previous letter dated 13th January (1868) was written by Basil Fanshawe over a number of days and the penultimate paragraph provides the date of closure as 15th January. The next letter to his mother is dated Monday 11th March 1868. This gap of nearly two months is significant but unexplained within the correspondence.

During that interval an event occurred that undoubtedly would cause Basil to communicate information to his family - but noticeably there are no letters for that period.

In the absence of a letter we have the words of the war correspondent George A Henty[1], who provides a powerful and vivid image of a tragedy that took place on 25th January 1868:

'Senafe, January 31st (1868)... On my arrival in camp I found that a deep gloom hung over everyone, and I heard the sad news that Colonel Dunn, the commanding officer of the 33d, had the day before accidentally shot himself when out shooting.

The native servant who alone was with him reports that he himself was at the moment stooping to pour out some water, that he heard the report of a gun, and turning round saw his master stagger back, and then sink into a

---

[1] 'The March to Magdala' by George A Henty 1832-1902 (Special Correspondent of the Standard) - Published 1868 (reproduced - www.gutenberg.org).

sitting position with the blood streaming from his breast. The man instantly ran back to camp, a distance of five miles, for assistance, and surgeons at once galloped off with bandages, followed by dhoolie wallahs[1], with a dhoolie[2] to carry him back to camp.

When the surgeons arrived, they found Colonel Dunn lying on his back, dead. His flask was open by his side, his cap pulled over his face. He had bled to death in a few minutes after the accident. It is supposed that the gun was at full cock, and that the slight jar of putting the butt to the ground must have let the hammer down.

There are very few men who could have been less spared than Colonel Dunn; none more deeply regretted. As an officer he was one of the most rising men in the service, and had he lived would probably have gained its highest honours and position. He was with the 11th Hussars in the Balaclava charge, and when the men were asked to select the man who in the whole regiment was most worthy of the Victoria Cross, they unanimously named Lieutenant Dunn. Never was the Victoria Cross placed on the breast of a more gallant soldier.

When the 100th regiment was raised in Canada, he enrolled a very large number of men, and was gazetted it's major. After attaining the rank of lieutenant-colonel he exchanged into the 33d, of which, at the time of this sad accident, he was full colonel, and was next on the list for his brigadier-generalship.

He was only thirty-five years of age, the youngest colonel in the British service, and would, in all human probability, have been a brigadier-general before he was thirty-six. Known as a dashing officer, distinguished for his personal bravery, a colonel at an age when other men are captains, there was no rank or position in the army which he might not have confidently

---

[1] An Indian dhoolie carrier.
[2] A bamboo or light stretcher to carry the sick or wounded.

been predicted to attain, and his loss is a loss to the whole British army. But not less than as a soldier, do all who knew poor Dunn regret him as a man. He was the most popular of officers. Unassuming, frank, kind-hearted in the extreme, a delightful companion, and a warm friend—none met him who were not irresistibly attracted by him. He was a man essentially to be loved. In his regiment his loss is irreparable, and as they stood beside his lonely grave at the foot of the rock of Senafe, it is no disgrace to their manhood to say that there were few dry eyes amongst either officers or men.

He was buried, in accordance with a wish he had once expressed, in his uniform, and Wolfe's lines on the burial of Sir John Moore will apply almost word for word to "the grave where our hero we buried."

The following extract from the Western Daily Press dated 29th February 1868 provides us with the opinion of the Court with regard to Colonel Dunn's death:

'The Fatal Accident to Col. Dunn.

Mr J Roberts Dunn, brother of the late Colonel Dunn V.C., 33rd Regiment, who was accidentally shot in Abyssinia, furnishes a brief account of the manner in which the accident occurred. He says; - "On the morning of the day of the accident my brother, accompanied by the surgeon of is regiment and six beaters, went for a day's shooting to the pass of Senafe.

In the afternoon, feeling fatigued, and fallen considerably in the rear of his companions, my brother sat down on some stones, his rifle resting on his left shoulder. In getting out his brandy flask his rifle must have slipped and come in violent contact with a stone, and one of the hammers (perfect in the morning) was found to have had its top broken off.

The opinion of the court is expressed in these words:- 'The Court, having carefully considered all the evidence before it, is of opinion that the death of Colonel Dunn was purely accidental, caused by his own rifle exploding while he was in the act of using his brandy flask when sitting on a stone out shooting.' I may add that I have frequently had occasion to remonstrate with my poor brother upon his extraordinary carelessness in the use of firearms"

That official cause of death given as 'Accidental' obviously satisfied both the Army and Colonel Dunn's family, but even at the time there were rumours and speculation which continues unabated even after more than 150 years. Obviously, Henty's description of Colonel Dunn highlights the romantic appeal of Canada's first heroic V.C, who came from a well -connected family in Toronto and was educated at Harrow School. Dunn had sold out his commission in the Hussars after the Crimean War and returned to Canada. There, instrumental in setting up the 100th Prince of Wales Royal Canadian Regiment, he served as Major. Later returning to England, he purchased into the 33rd Duke of Wellington's Regiment and was soon promoted to Colonel.

Although Alexander Dunn's Army career was extremely successful he had complicated his domestic life by running off with the wife of a brother officer in 11th Hussars. The lady's husband refused to divorce her but she remained with Dunn on his estate in Canada. Despite this indiscretion as Henty confirms, Dunn remained popular with the men of the 33rd for his courageous action in The Charge of the Light Brigade. They held him in high esteem and with his easy manner and unusually lean height of 6'3", he cut a dashing figure.

That reputation and the uncertainty of the truth of the way he died, have contributed towards the speculation of 'conspiracy theorists' who even today consider something more sinister than 'an accident' occurred to Dunn. Was his death deliberate and in revenge for the cuckolded husband? Did a manservant kill him to benefit from a recently changed will? What about his mistress, was his recent will changed to favour his sister and not her?

Colonel Alexander Dunn VC
33rd Duke of Wellington's Regiment
Wikicommons

Grave and memorial of Colonel Alexander Dunn VC
Senafe, Abyssinia (present day Eritrea)
Duke of Wellington's Regiment Trustees

Most of those issues are pertinent but how can we know if they played any part in his death? Nevertheless, it is probably the case that Basil Fanshawe had an opinion and by following carefully his comments we see that he briefly touches on the subject, leaving an impression…

His letter before the event makes several observations - he states that he shares a tent with Colonel Dunn, he advises that although he and others have recently suffered from diarrhoea, specifically the Colonel 'had a touch of fever' - but gives no cause. Colonel Dunn must have been quite ill in some way as Basil tells his mother that he has taken over command 'lots to do as Commanding Officer pro tem'.

Basil's first letter after the death of Colonel Dunn confirms he has received 3 letters from his mother in February but doesn't mention sending any to her. He confirms sending a letter to his older brother John, so perhaps we can speculate that with such a shockingly graphic story to relate he sent the details and his opinion to his brother?

As if to confirm his own doubts that the truth might not be reported, Basil's comments in that same very long letter, that there are conflicting opinions in the camp…

'I wrote to Uncle Tom from Senefe and asked if he would find out anything about poor Dunn's death & the stress being given in the Rgt. Opinions in camp vary – most think it is a toss-up and depends upon the interest brought to bear on the Horse Guards'.

The decision concerning the official cause of Dunn's death had obviously been concluded back in London as early as 29th February

1868. No doubt his family were consoled with the 'accidental death' verdict because once the possibility of foul play had been ruled out the only other alternative was 'suicide'. Such a verdict would have not only brought shame on the illustrious career of a brilliant young army officer, but also on his family. The act of suicide[1] was a crime in the nineteenth century and was viewed very differently than today. Poor mental health and depression had yet to be fully understood.

Could it be that Alexander Dunn whom Henty described as 'the youngest Colonel in the British Army' had a crisis of confidence? Beset by an off balance moment perhaps caused by poor health and stress, with whom could he share his thoughts within that masculine environment? Fanshawe tells of shared cold sleepless nights under canvas with Dunn – isn't it strange that there is not a word of his evidence in the official records?

Alexander Dunn VC has a grave in a lonely spot in Abyssinia (Eritrea). During the last 150 years it has at times been lost, found and unreachable due to war and conflict, yet via the internet, his name and story live on to enthral and intrigue.

---

[1] Only decriminalised in Great Britain as late as 1961.

Written by Thomas Basil Fanshawe - to his Mother.
Camp Antalo
Monday March 11th (18)68

My dearest Mother,

I had no time on arriving here on Saturday last to write more than a hurried line to Minnie to ask her to inform you that I was here & all well. The mail left that night for Youlla and I had no more time so I will try now by saying that I received yours of the 2nd, 10th & 18th all right & many thanks for the same. I am always delighted to hear from you. I delivered the letter to Col. or rather General Mereweather[1] Mrs May gave you, in person myself yesterday. He was very civil & I found he knew Blanche[2] & Tiny[3] Le M, they having passed thro' Aden when he was Resident there. I do not suppose he will be able to do anything for me – but time may show.

I will begin about our march here & myself first. The last letter I wrote was to John, Feb'y 23rd No. 4 – and I left Senafe on the 25th. I told you about the march I made to Attegerat in one of my former letters so won't repeat except to say that we reached Attegerat on the 27th, halted there on 28th and proceeded on route here on the 29th. I had just time for a hurried scrawl to Minnie at that place – as I was fully employed nearly every hour of my stay there. Everyone's kit

---

[1] Major General Sir William Lockyer Merewether KCSI, CB (1825–1880) was the British Resident at Aden from 1863 to 1867. When the problem in Abyssinia occurred he led an advance party seeking the best military entrance into the Uplands and he identified the way through the Tekonda Pass to Senafe. After the successful expedition to Magdala he was promoted to Brigadier General.
[2] TBF's cousin Blanche Maude Le Marchant daughter of Sir Gaspard Le Marchant.
[3] TBF's cousin, Clementina Mary Meysey Le Marchant, daughter of General Sir John Gaspard Le Marchant married in 1869, Maj-Gen. Hon. Edward Archibald Brabazon Acheson (1844-1921) younger brother of 4th Earl of Gosford.

being cut down to 75 lbs weight, including everything and the soldiers to 25lb. I have brought nothing on but a carpet bag & my bedding - no bedstead - & a copper basin trimmed with a leather cover which contained the whole of my washing and toilet arrangements. My guns I had to leave behind, one at Senefe & one at Attegerat. I suppose I shall get them again when we go back, if all goes well – my cooking *e 24*) pots go on a pass mule as we are allowed one to every 6 officers – and as our brandy is drunk, I hope to be able to carry my horse gear on one – tables & chairs out of the question. I only regret my guns & powder shot we left behind. The advantages is that not much packing is required of a morning.

We left Attegerat about 9.30 on 27th Feby & had a long heavy march about 14 miles to Mai Wondaj – water good – the only accommodation, the tents were so saturated with too heavy dew that morning, we were obliged to wait for them to dry or the mules would have broken down under the weight.

Just before leaving I got two letters, one from Minnie & yourself dated 10th Feby & very glad I was to find that Minnie & the chicks had arrived all right & that you had been kind enough to have taken them in for the night. She would have gone to an hotel unless you had taken compassion on her. You must have had a good squeeze. Many thanks for so doing & I hope you were not much inconvenienced on their account.

We left Mai Wondaj (Mai means river) a little brook about a foot broad & two inches deep – which they dignified with the name of rivers & got to Ada Bargir on March the 1st – up one hill, then down & up again – about 15 miles – a longer march and harder than the previous day, and the Artillery must have some trouble descending a long and very steep hill. All the road has been made by our men

Troops in the Gorge – the Devil's Staircase
Duke of Wellington's Regiment Trustees

Antalo Church

working parties. The natives do not seem to care about roads when made. From Ada Bargir to Dongollo on 2nd March a nice short march of 8 miles - lots of water & every one enjoying a bath in the pools & water melons which we looked upon as a great luxury. Here, we got for the first time, the native bread, made of barley meal, about the size of the oatcakes you used to have made in former days, but about an inch thick, not bad eating and a great improvement upon Commissariat biscuit – now the Corps Department Office, the bread to the men. When we first find a ration, troops come thro' – one got 14 or 16 for the dollar[1] and you are lucky to buy 8 or 10 – the natives won't look at anything under a dollar and dispute the rupee in toto. I also bought some fish there, about 12 – 15 for half a dollar. I do not know how my servant got that coin. The fish made a change, eaten like carp & full of bones but better than nothing. Nesbitt[2] of ours and Bainbridge[3] of Land Transport took a walk about 4 o'clock in afternoon & got 8 hares & 5 brace of spun fowl, rather a different species to any I have yet come across. Nesbitt kindly let me have a shot or two with his gun – I got 4 spun fowl & missed two hares – the gun not quite suiting me.

From Dongollo we marched to Agula (*added* March 4th) a nice short march, & I halted a day to mend some mule gear. At Dongollo but was not lucky enough & lost my only good line with me – nearly rotten though it was. I have a few hooks left. Plenty of water at Agula & a very stony encamping ground.

---

[1] Generally accepted term for 5 shillings sterling.

[2] Lt. Edward Nesbitt – enlisted as Ensign 1853, retired as Major - after 1888.

[3] Captain Bainbridge, Land Transport Corps –'who had the very difficult duty of providing water for the troops throughout the operations since leaving the Bashilo River'. (Dispatch - Major General Staveley Commanding 1st Division Abyssinia Field Force - London Gazette June 16th 1868).

On the 5th March - a long days walk of 15 miles, of course up & down hill & stiff ones to Bolo River, on the 6th from Bolo River to Hay Kalla (*added* 9 miles) & in here on the 7th about 12 miles – at Bolo River I saw some of the finest trees I have yet seen, a species of Indian fig tree & picked buttercups, wild roses & jessamine. Saw two couple snipe, but only having big shot in Nesbitt's gun, did not get a crack at them. I shot a guinea fowl, the only shot I had and could not get him.

If I have been interrupted once, since the top of this page, I suppose I must have had twenty or more on all sorts of subjects, being in command of this Left Wing, so I will stop for the day as I cannot write a line without being distracted on some folly or other. An Orderly comes to ones tent about every five minutes with ("<u>Chittie Elya Sahib</u>") – English, "brought a note, Sir" – here's another so I stop till tomorrow!

Thursday March 11th – we got in here on Saturday, about 10 o'clock. Lots of water & no end of stones. The Comm. In Chief & Sir C. Stavely were here – we found our H^D Quarter Wing all right and thought they were waiting for us to go on to the point but they left on Monday last, leaving me with the Left Wing here.

I heard from Holland[1] (*added* Quartermaster General Department) this morning, that he thought another four days would see us Left Wing out of this. I hope so – Sir R Napier & H^D Quarter Staff & Sir C Stavely, and the whole of the 4th, a battery of steel guns and the Balooches have gone on today. 40 Elephants came in yesterday, they

---

[1] Lt. Colonel Trevenen James Holland C.B., Bombay Staff (1836 - 1910) Quartermaster General to Sir Robert Napier and mentioned in dispatches.

are to carry the Armstrong guns[1] of Murray's battery[2] and I suppose it will fall to our lot to escort them. Letters were received two or three days back from the Prisoners at Magdala. Up to 17th of last month all well! The report is that Theodore has entrenched himself & is waiting our arrival, this I very much doubt but quite wide awake enough to come down on us at any unguarded moment or spot should he think he would catch us. I fancy he won't show much fight in the open. Sir R.E. Napier is to be at Magdala on the 1st April – we shall see. No end of supplies here and I hear a strong brigade is on its way to be stationed here and set free the troops now here. A Captain Speedy[3] whom I met here, formerly in Theodore's Army, before that in our 81st Rgt, told me that Theodore's army consisted of about 800 men on ponies, 800 men armed with guns & about 1000 spear men.

I hope it may all be over soon as it is not very comfortable work, the country does not improve as we get further into it, though it may. Uphill, downhill varied with grass plains about 2 or three miles long & half as much broad in the valleys between the hills. The town of Antalo or village, is quite 5 or 7 miles from here. I have not been there & doubt very much if I shall. C.Os are all in the beastly single fly bell tents. The double fly are much better. These are little or no

---

[1] Designed by Sir William Armstrong and manufactured from 1855 at Elswick Ordnance Co these were an original design of rifled breech-loading field and heavy gun with a built-up gun construction system of a wrought-iron (but by 1868, mild steel tubing) surrounded by multiple wrought-iron strengthening coils shrunk over the inner tube to keep it under compression.

[2] A reference to the artillery battery located on Battery Path, beneath Government Hill in Central Hong Kong to protect colonial headquarters. Named after Sir George Murray and built in 1841.

[3] Captain Tristram C. S. Speedy (1839 – 1911) - explorer and adventurer who served in King Theodore's army sometime before 1868. His knowledge of Abyssinia was crucial to Sir Robert Napier during the expedition. Later Queen Victoria appointed him guardian to Prince Alamayou, Theodore's son.

protection from the sun, and the only way is to put up about a foot of the canvas nearest the ground & lie down. I had one tent to myself but took in our Doctor Steel[1] who is attached to us, lots of room for two with only 75lbs allowed, but three is rather a tight fit.

Collings has to remain here in command of this brigade and station, much to his disgust as he hoped to get on to the front. Cooper is looking very well and all the better for marching. Nothing has yet been heard from England about Col. Dunn's (state) yet. In fact you will know more about it than we shall & sooner. John might be able to find out what the powers that be intend to do in the matter?

We find it much warmer at night & in the day but a strong wind gets up at nine or 10 o'clock and covers everything with dust.

I suppose we ought to have another mail in soon – we get one generally, once a week. To show how uncertain they are I will tell you when I got your last written Feby 10th on the 29th at Attejerat, the one of Feby 2nd on March 7th on arriving here & the one of Feby 18th on March 8th.

You seem to have been quite gay at the Russell's, going out to dances & dinners. I recollect the Frys[2] who used to live at the Vicarage but cannot say I remember much of the daughters. I will send a line if possible to Mrs Russell & thank her for the letter, but I have so much to do that I cannot promise. Among other trifles, two

---

[1] Dr W H Steele, Royal Artillery attached to 33rd Regiment.

[2] Most probably Mrs Fanshawe referred to the family of Joseph Fry who lived at Fairkytes, Hornchurch, son of the Quaker social reformer Elizabeth Fry, who resided at Barking. Joseph Fry is listed in the 1871 Census as a Magistrate and merchant who was stated as born in 1809. The daughters mentioned in 1868 were Ruth (19) and Margaret (21).

or three times a day the grass round camp gets on fire and we have to turn all the men out to extinguish it – a great nuisance!

I was very pleased to get your letter of Feby 10th, which I got before Minnie's of the same date at Attejerat and found she had arrived all right. I don't wonder at her looking ill & thin with all the bother & worry she has had the last two or three months – I hope she will give up Gerard more to the nurse, and that he himself will soon get easy & strong. Mr Gosselin sent me a line by the last mail, they do not think Minnie looking well or improved by India. Wonder if they did!

Minnie says she does not consider May as pretty as described & I am afraid that the young lady won't approve of divided attention. I am sorry Master Gerard was so unsociable with you – we thought he was a pretty little chap in India but I suppose besides English children he looks pale & delicate. I hope Minnie will get someone to assist in the nursery, the only difficulty being where & how to dispose of another servant if they remain in 28 Park Street and I don't suppose Mrs G will let Minn go away unless the three children are too much for Mr Gosselin, now he is confined to his house or rather was, for I hope long before this he was about again. Minn says she finds him much aged and his eyes worse. Lizzie & Mrs G - much as she left them, the baby is wonderfully improved both in looks and temper so Minnie says, but no doubt I am telling you what you know already.

Minnie says you want her to pay you a visit, I am afraid the three chicks, if they came would be too much of an infliction on you and I do not think she knows how to separate any of them, perhaps between you, you will be able to devise some means of meeting. I am sure Minnie must be delighted to get out of India, which I know she hated as much as I did. If her report is correct she did pretty well with our sale at Karachee as nearly £150 was placed to her credit in the Agra Bank[1], after paying for her expenses home. This is better than I expected & am glad she postponed the sale till after her departure & the arrival of the 82nd Rgt[2]. In Karachee. I thought we should have lost a good deal, but if correct, have done well, but of course not made anything. This included carriage & crockery we took out with us.

You ask me if I have seen many rare animals - except deer & monkeys I have seen none! Great big fellows the latter, as big as donkeys – baboons, in fact. Lots of fine eagles, hawks, green pigeons[3] & small birds, but I could not waste powder or shot nor carry them. If I get back all right, I will bring some home. I have sent John yesterday and am sending another packet of florican[4] feathers which I hope will prove acceptable & arrive all safe. My horse continues well but very thin from the reduced rations he now gets. I think I told you that now only mounted officers are allowed native (grass xxxxx), all private native servants are sent back, belonging to everyone.

I am quite well, much better than ever I was in India. The constant exercise & open air, the cause I fancy. This is a capital climate, what I

---

[1] Agra Bank Ltd - reformed in 1867 from the previous Agra & United Services Bank later Agra & Masterman's Bank, an Indian-based British overseas bank with clients mainly from the military and government services.

[2] 82nd (Prince of Wales's Volunteers) Regiment.

[3] A bird in the pigeon family, (Treron), widely known as green pigeon. With a natural habitat in woodland areas across Asia and Africa the birds have characteristic green bodies due to a diet of fruit, nuts and seeds and each of the 29 species have a variety of different colour plumage.

[4] The Kori Bustard (Ardeotis Kori) the largest flying bird native to southern and eastern Africa The male Kori Bustard may be the heaviest living animal capable of flight and may stand nearly 4ft tall with a wingspan of up to 9ft.

have seen at present, or rather would be if one had a house to live and not bell tent.

When I have not time to write to anyone of you in town, I have told Minn to send you word if she hears by the post & you do not.

I fancy from your last that Blanche has been married before this if everything has gone right. It seems a queer match and hope it will turn out well. What an absurdity, Johnny trying to enter the Army without money. His parents seem to take the whole affair uncommonly easy & not bother much about it. I suppose the house[1] is mainly furnished now that Sir G has taken – no doubt settled in it. I wonder what Johnny will turn to at last?

I got your copy of Dick's letters, many thanks for it, have you heard again? & satisfactory if you have?

The tenant at Parsloes seems to have done wonders. I wish I could accompany you when you pay your 'talked of' visit there this summer.

Thank Helen for hers of Feby 3rd, how changed they must have found White Hill[2]! Nellie[3] I hope enjoyed her ball, I suppose she does a deal of going out now. Minnie says she thought Helen

---

[1] On his death 6th February 1874, Sir J G Le Marchant's address was 80 St Georges' Square, Pimlico.

[2] Denison House, the country residence of Helen Denison at Little Gaddesden, Hertfordshire where she lived to the age of 91. The property had a beautiful garden and conservatories where Helen and her head gardener Arthur Gentle propagated new strains of Sweet Pea, achieving great success at the Royal Horticultural Society national shows.

[3] Helen's eldest child, Helen Jemima Denison (1845 – 1889) - she married her cousin's widower William Romilly, 2nd Baron Romilly in 1872.

looking particularly well. I wrote to Uncle Tom[1] from Senefe and asked if he would find out anything about poor Dunn's death & the stress being given in the Rgt. Opinions in camp vary – most think it is a toss up and depends upon the interest brought to bear on the Horse Guards. I am stopped, so goodbye for today.

Saturday March 14th – not much news, another mountain train battery came in this morning & I believe we are to go on Monday or early in the week, on the front. The dust is beastly here & wind very strong – which blows everything about in a fitting manner. The sooner we are out of this the better – it is the worse camp I have had the misfortune to be in!

I sent John 1 packet of feathers direct & another to Minnie, which she is to send on. I will keep my eye open to procure more. I have received the "Times" newspapers all right up to this. They are a great luxury, thanks to you or John for executing my commission. I am called off on duty so will bring this to a conclusion with best love to you all - and the same to yourself ever dearest Mother.

Your most affectionate son
Basil

A mail is expected today but of course, has not arrived yet. We had the grass on fire again yesterday & owing to a strong wind the men could not put it out, it beat them altogether and it burnt all night & looked very grand. Thank Mrs Russell & Mrs May for the letter to Mereweather – tell Margaret I asked after her and am glad to find that she admires the boys.

---

[1] Colonel Thomas Le Marchant (1811 – 1873) – youngest brother of TBF's mother, he served in the Military and Naval Intelligence Service.

Once more goodbye – you will be surprised to find my name in full on envelope but am told it is necessary as it saves postage. Let me know if this correct?

Written by Thomas Basil Fanshawe - to his brother John Gaspard
Fanshawe
Camp Dalanta Plain
Tuesday April 21st 1868

My dearest John,

We have had so much hard work & marching that till within the last few days I have had no time to write to anyone except a line to Minnie. We have had a very rough time of it the last few weeks. At a place called Sildee all our baggage was reduced from 75lbs to what mounted officers could carry on their horses and as one had to ride the horse besides, the allowance was not great, a blanket & a greatcoat about all. Luckily, Sinclair, Cooper & self, have lived in a hospital tent but liable to turn out at any moment in the event of any sick coming in – officers 12 in a tent. No grog[1], no sugar & hardly anything but meal biscuit & tea.

We have had some terrific marching – one day on rear guard, I left camp about 2 in the afternoon & did not get in to next camp here, till about the same time the following day. I was with Murray's guns which were on elephants & it came on to rain & made the road so bad that the poor devils could not move – one of them fell & blocked up the road & the others would not attempt it, so we had to wait till next morning. We fortunately managed to light a big fire & sit around till morning. It rained at one time that night, about as hard as I ever recollect.

We arrived here about Thursday week & had our first view of Magdala, the next day Good Friday we went down to the Bastulo

---

[1] Regulation rum ration diluted with water as drunk in the Royal Navy but in this situation probably related only to alcoholic drink of any type.

Elephants carrying artillery at Tekeze River
Wikicommons

The burning fortress of Magdala after the British Expeditionary Force defeated Tewodros II

Illustrated London News - Wikicommons

River, ours being the second Brigade, the 1st going on the reconnoitre & Theodore sent his men out to attack. They got awfully chewed up. The steel guns & snipers doing great execution and sweeping the natives down like rats. We were married up that night to the 2nd Brigade expecting to be attacked again the next morning, but were not, though fully prepared.

We employed that day Saturday, in burying the native dead, about 370 & I believe that 2000 was the amount of killed or wounded. This so sickened them & frighten Theodore that he sent in to treat and on Sunday the whole of the prisoners were sent in alive & well. Our loss on Friday was about 12 men wounded in the 1st Brigade – ours was not engaged.

Theodore's army got it so hot & heavy that they would not fight any more. On Monday, after having refused to come in (Theodore) which was the only condition on which Sir R Napier would treat, we proceeded to go into Magdala - one of the strangest place to take, that man ever wished to see. First of all a hill called Falah then another hill called Islangi & behind, Magdala. If properly defended we should have had a heavy loss.

We got to Islangi without a shot being fired, the natives having all laid down their arms. Theodore was in Magdala and determined to fight it out, so after shelling it a bit we advanced, our regiment leading – about two o'clock. A very nasty place to get into, one gun in position would have swept us down by scores, not one in twenty would have escaped, a nearly perpendicular rock to ascend with an abatis[1] all round. The gate was (imxxxxable) & we had to climb over the stockade to the right.

There was about 9000 men In Magdala that morning but I believe they bolted at the first shell and not above 100 desolate men were fighting – inside there was another gate & stockade, about 25 yards inside the first gate. Our sniders[2] are a beautiful weapon and nothing would stand against their one continuous roar – no delay in loading.

We had five men wounded, all doing well – one a sergeant was shot in the leg not two feet me, on the road in – a narrow shave. Once in, there was very little more fighting. Theodore shot himself, put a pistol to his mouth & the balls came out of the back of his head. He was a determined looking ruffian, with rather a hooked nose, eaten up by conceit that he was the only Emperor in the world & his knowledge of fighting confined to the tribes in his country, who when he fired his guns, all ran away & he expected us to do the same. I was very much impressed that our men stood either still or advanced.

He was a great fool to give up the Prisoners without coming to terms – no doubt he fancied that was all we wanted & he thought we should be satisfied. Altogether you may put it down as a most wonderful success & the biggest fluke at the same time. The 1st Brigade were particularly ordered not to fight that day & they did –

---

[1] A field fortification creating an obstacle - usually branches of trees laid in a rows with the sharpened tops directed outwards and towards the enemy then usually interwoven or tied with wire or other obstacles.

[2] The British .577 Snider–Enfield - a breech-loading rifle adopted by the British Army in 1866 and used until the end of the 19th century. Deployed for the first time at the Battle of Magdala, it is recorded that the 4th (King's Own) Regiment of Foot fired as many as 10,200 rounds.

if it had not been for the dressing they (*added* natives) got then we should have had a heavy loss from them firing down on us - & we thank our stars that we were so well out of it.

Every European prisoner released, alive and well, Theodore killed, his army dispersed & our loss only one man who died from wounds received on Friday – one of two Punjarbees.

We remained in Magdala that night, sleeping on the ground, having found an old tent which we lay on & pulled part over us. We had nothing to eat except what we looted – eggs, fowls & sheep, water – very little and that as black as ink.

Nothing very valuable in the shape of loot, some of our men got a heap of dollars – none of which I was lucky enough to come across. Those who got dollars were allowed to keep them but everything else was ordered to be given up. I had a very handsome state dress of Theodore's but was obliged to return it. The sale of things found at Magdala took place here yesterday and the prices fetched were enormous. There was a gold chalice and gold crown which I should have liked to have had but Holmes[1] who is out here for the British Museum got them for it.

We remained at Magdala till Wednesday afternoon – the 4th relieving us much to their disgust. Went to Hd Quarters Camp about

---

[1] Richard Holmes, an assistant in the department of manuscripts at the British Museum, removed a number of objects - manuscripts, regalia, religious antiquities and other material - from the imperial treasury and from the Church of the Saviour of the World. Holmes also made a sketch of the face of the dead King Theodore which was reproduced in the British press. A golden crown and chalice initially acquired by Holmes from a soldier were deposited in the V & A Museum by H.M. Treasury in 1872.

6 miles from Magdala, next day to Bashilo River & on here Friday where the whole force have since joined us.

I did not get a wash from the time of leaving the Bashilo River till I got back & never changed any clothes all the time – now nothing to change, all baggage being left behind. Our Regiment did all the work that was to be done on the Monday - & did it well.

We had a parade of the whole troops yesterday morning and Sir R. N. made a good speech & Thesiger[1] read out a very complementary general order. The opinion here is that they will make Sir R N a peer & give the troops a medal[2] with clasp for Magdala six months later and some will get brevets[3]. I only hope all this is true or will be. There is also a talk of Persia giving the troops a medal on account of the number of Prisoners belonging to Persia. I have seen very little

---

[1] Frederic Augustus Thesiger, 2nd Baron Chelmsford GCB, GCVO (1827 –1905) Deputy adjutant general, in the 1868 Expedition to Abyssinia and awarded Companion of the Bath, made an aide-de-camp to Queen Victoria in 1868. Adjutant-General India from 1869 to 1874. Came to prominence during the Anglo-Zulu War, when an expeditionary force of his command suffered one of the severest defeats in battle in the history of the British Empire at the Battle of Isandlwana in 1879 but later defeated the Zulu Kingdom at the subsequent Battle of Ulundi.

[2] Established 1st March 1869 the Abyssinan medal was awarded to participants in the campaign from 4th October 1867 to 19 April 1868. A circular silver medal suspended from a crown and ribbon of crimson with white borders. The face of the medal depicts Queen Victoria wearing a diadem and has an ornate surround. The reverse has a wreath border surrounding a centre where the recipient's name is individually engraved.

[3] An officer promotion awarded for outstanding service but without the pay of the full higher rank –e.g. Brevet Major.

Sir Richard Rivington Holmes (1835–1911)
Assistant in the manuscript department at the British Museum
1870 – Librarian, Windsor Castle.
Illustrated London News - Wikicommons

33rd Regiment at the Magdala Sentry Post

of the released Prisoners, I believe Rassam[1] is a great ruffian &
Cameron[2] a drunkard.

We go down today to the Pooo River & expect to be at Senefe about
23rd of next month. There was a beastly report yesterday afloat that
there was a chance of our going home round the Cape, I hope no
truth in it, it would be a sell and sixty days the shortest time we
could do it in.

I am afraid Dunn's step will not be given in the Reg't, rather a sell
for Lacy. Cooper is all right and I get on very well with him but I
think he does not get on very well with superiors. Collings has been
left behind at Autelo which won't please him. I believe he is seedy &
will never be surprised if he goes on h.p.[3] – Cooper looks as fit as
possible.

We have had hardly any sickness among the troops,
notwithstanding their hard work and having to carry greatcoats,
waterproof sheets & blanket on their backs on the March – and they
deserve all they may get for the hard work & short commons they
have had. It will be better going back as we shall pull back on our
supplies. I can assume if we have had a very tough time of it the last
three weeks. If we go home via Suez we shall be home D.V. about
the end of June or early in July - & thank God when we shall be in
England again!

---

[1] Hormuzd Rassam (1826 –1910) an Assyrian archeologist who was a Christian and
later became British by naturalization. Captured by Theodore whilst attempting to
broker the release of the existing prisoners when acting as a British diplomat.
[2] Charles Duncan Cameron (died 1870) was a British soldier who was serving as
British consul in Ethiopia when he was imprisoned by Theodore.
[3] Half-Pay - the pay or allowance an officer received when in retirement or not in
actual service.

I have not got the parcel you kindly sent out, perhaps may pick it up on the road somewhere. We had two hail storms on this plain & the stones were quite as big as marbles & made you jump when they hit you. We had one in Magdala, not quite so heavy but it was very acceptable as it afforded us a supply of drinking water.

Minnie in her last says that you wrote about her passage money home. It is very kind of you taking the trouble & hope you may succeed but I am doubtful. When I get back to Senefe I will try to get Dunn's grave photographed & send you a copy. I now hear (*added above* Friends) want (*added above* us) to take his body home.

Paper & time say stop as we march at 2 o'clock. Love to Bab & the chicks, & same to my Mother & Helen, to whom you can show this.

We have a long job before us, 32 marches to Zoulla - I wish it was over & well out of the country.

Now goodbye & believe me your ever affectionate brother,

Basil

Magdala was burnt to the ground & all the guns burnt. No doubt you will have seen a full account in the papers of our proceedings, before this reaches you.

Index

Departure of the British Expeditionary Force from Magdala
Illustrated London News 1868

Index

Abyssinia War Medal 1868 - Silver
Duke of Wellington's Regiment Trustees

The Archives & Local Studies Centre at Valence House Museum in the London Borough of Barking & Dagenham is the source and inspiration for many local heritage projects. When volunteers working there wish to develop and expand topics of significant local historical interest they are encouraged with the generous support of the professional staff.

This publication is part of the legacy that has followed after a successful Heritage Lottery Project based upon the publication in 2016 of Thomas Basil Fanshawe's Crimean War letters. Hopefully, next year we will publish Basil's final collection of letters from Colonial India.

The transcriber and editor wish to thank their fellow volunteers and Valence House staff for their patience and interest in this project. Scott Flaving of DWR Trustees must be thanked for his continued helpful advice regarding military matters. We appreciate his friendship and support.

Our greatest thanks will always go to John Gordon, for trusting us with the freedom to interpret his Fanshawe family treasures and for showing his pleasure in all our efforts to tell the Fanshawe story.

Praise

The Soul of a Dog dismantles reductionist behaviorism with rare intellectual courage. Tsai's analysis of consciousness, time perception, and psychosomatic dysfunction forces our field to confront what we've ignored for decades: dogs are not conditioned machines, but sentient family systems.
Aaron Poynton | Bestselling Author, *Think Like a Black Sheep*

The Soul of a Dog is an enlightening read that deepened my understanding of consciousness across all forms of life. Tsai's ideas and observations have the potential to reshape how we interpret human behavior in the era of artificial intelligence.
Kumar Parakala | Chairman, Thriveco, USA National Bestselling Author, *Lead to Disrupt*

I went in skeptical. I came out questioning everything I'd been taught. Tsai's success with genuinely predatory dogs without force or correction is impossible to dismiss.
Hans Lagerweij | CEO, Flying Dutchman Consultancy, Author of *Why Whisperer*

This book gave me something no training manual ever has—hope. Tsai's compassionate rehabilitation of dogs deemed "unadoptable" reframes shelters not as endpoints, but as moral responsibilities humanity has failed to uphold.
Tamara Nall | CEO & Founder, The Leading Niche

ISBN 978-1-63735-277-9 (hcv)
ISBN 978-1-63735-276-2 (pbk)
ISBN 978-1-63735-278-6 (ebook)

Library of Congress Control Number: 2025928161